FOR

I THINK YOU'D ENJOY THIS BOOK BECAUSE

FROM

PRINCIPLES FOR THE NEXT CENTURY OF WORK

Sense & Respond Press publishes short, beautiful, actionable books on topics related to innovation, digital transformation, product management, and design. Our readers are smart, busy, practical innovators. Our authors are experts working in the fields they write about.

The goal of every book in our series is to solve a real-world problem for our readers. Whether that be understanding a complex and emerging topic, or something as concrete (and difficult) as hiring innovation leaders, our books help working professionals get better at their jobs, quickly.

Jeff Gothelf & Josh Seiden

Series co-editors **Jeff Gothelf** and **Josh Seiden** wrote *Lean UX* (O'Reilly) and *Sense & Respond* (Harvard Business Review Press) together. They were co-founding principals of Neo Innovation (sold to Pivotal Labs) in New York City and helped build it into one of the most recognized brands in modern product strategy, development, and design. In 2017 they were short-listed for the Thinkers50 award for their contributions to innovation leadership. Learn more about Jeff and Josh at www.jeffgothelf.com and www.joshseiden.com.

OTHER BOOKS FROM SENSE & RESPOND PRESS

Lean vs. Agile vs. Design Thinking
What you really need to know to build high-performing digital product teams
Jeff Gothelf

Making Progress
The 7 responsibilities of the innovation leader
Ryan Jacoby

Hire Women
An agile framework for hiring and retaining women in technology
Debbie Madden

The Invisible Leader (forthcoming)
Facilitation secrets for catalyzing change, cultivating innovation, and commanding results
Elena Astilleros

What CEOs Need To Know About Design (forthcoming)
Using design to grow revenue and maximize strategic impact
Audrey Crane

HIRING FOR THE INNOVATION ECONOMY

Issued in print and electronic formats.
ISBN 978-0-9994769-8-7 (ebook)
ISBN 978-0-9994769-9-4 (paperback)
ISBN 978-1-7239005-4-9 (KDP paperback)

Editor: Victoria Olsen
Designer: Mimi O Chun
Interior typesetting: Jennifer Blais

Published in the United States by Sense & Respond Press
www.senseandrespondpress.com

Printed and bound in the United States.
1 2 3 4 20 19 18 17

Nicole Rufuku

HIRING FOR THE INNOVATION ECONOMY

Three steps to improve performance and diversity

SENSE & RESPOND PRESS

INTRODUCTION: YOUR TEAM IS YOUR DESTINY

Hiring has always been a high priority for managers. But in today's innovation economy, hiring has become the single most important responsibility managers have. For teams building the future, hiring isn't just another administrative task—it's the competitive advantage that will separate the winners from the rest.

As business practices and technologies evolve, the resources that were important in the past are now commoditized. Gone are the days when you could establish competitive advantage with state-of-the-art equipment, design, marketing, or technology. Although expensive and necessary, these inputs are now easily replicated by well-funded competitors.

The one thing competitors can't copy? Your people and teams. Even in the most cutting edge spaces, it's the layer of human insight and ingenuity that drives the success of innovation in the new economy. The people you hire will decide how to build, customize, and apply today's readily available edge technology to create something truly impactful. Those people will also create the culture that nurtures and sustains continued innovation. Mediocre teams sometimes get lucky and build winning products. But the teams that perform exceptionally and innovate over the long run have one thing in common: they hire better than the competition.

WHAT'S WRONG WITH THE WAY WE HIRE TODAY?

A couple of years ago, I was in the market for a new job. I was looking for a leadership role in product management at a growing startup. I was eager to explore exciting opportunities in New York City, where fascinating ideas and business models were getting funding. Unfortunately, the experience didn't live up to my expectations. So many smart, innovative teams put me through interview processes that were disorganized, unfocussed, and downright disrespectful. It was clear to me that many interviewers were winging it and hadn't thought through their questions. When it took companies a long time to follow-up with me, it was usually because they were confused about the type of person they needed—so they dragged their feet hoping to delay a decision they weren't prepared to make. One company got halfway through the interview process before they realized they no longer needed the position as it was defined. I was dumbfounded. How could such smart, competent people do this so poorly? But when I thought back to my own experiences hiring, I knew I was guilty of the same failures.

I could have ignored these experiences and moved on. But because I've spent so many years of my career searching for and tackling interesting challenges, it's difficult for me to see urgent, high-stakes problems without digging in and exploring them. Although I started my career at Microsoft initially focused on product strategy, I've spent the last decade focused on early-stage product development. I built digital businesses from ideation to scale with entrepreneurs, non-profits and Fortune 500 companies. For me, one of the most intoxicating experiences is identifying a new and urgent problem ripe for exciting new solutions.

So, of course, I couldn't help myself.

I dove into research and data to find the evidence on job interview methodology. In 2016, I also talked with and conducted an online survey of hiring managers and job applicants to understand the extent of the problem. After hearing from 108 U.S. hiring managers, Chief Operating Officers, and people executives, I realized the problems are surprisingly consistent, and the impact is profound.

To tackle these challenges, I decided to translate the proven best practices for hiring into practical tools for busy managers. Most practices that significantly improve hiring are extremely complex and almost impossible to implement in a fast-paced environment. So I simplified them to their essential components. In this redesign, I also leveraged the innovation principles I've used to lead teams in the development of digital products: creative brainstorming, collaboration, data-driven improvement, and transparency. I borrowed these tools from the product development world because they represent a commitment to innovation through open and continuous collaboration. If your team is building the future, these principles should be baked into all the ways you work, including (and especially) hiring. These principles are the most basic components of a creative culture: they are the DNA of innovation.

The first underlying issue with hiring I identified is that companies don't have a consistent and scalable process. Hiring is ad hoc, completely improvised from manager to manager. Another issue is that companies don't capture data related to the job interview and hiring process. In fact, in my 2016 online survey, 22% of hiring managers admitted they need to create more consistency in their hiring process, and only 18% said they track hiring data to improve their hiring process. As a result, they don't know which hiring practices work and which don't, and they are therefore unable to improve their results. Finally, companies don't train and prepare their teams to hire. Eighty-eight percent of survey respondents admitted they were not even made aware of the most basic guidelines for interviewing, such as which interview topics to avoid due to state and federal laws. Employees with varying levels of experience are thrown into interviews with little guidance and instruction. So they make it up and improvise. Is it any surprise that only 17% of job candidates reported encountering well-managed hiring experiences? There is a massive opportunity for smart companies to improve the way they hire and win the talent race by making hiring a competitive advantage.

NO PROCESS: HOW JOB INTERVIEWS UNDERMINE YOUR DIVERSITY GOALS

Seventy-eight percent of companies I surveyed let job interviews and hiring experiences simply happen, trusting and hoping that this critical process will naturally evolve into an effective methodology for evaluating candidates. Ad hoc decisions are made in real-time, and people infuse their own personal touch.

Job interviews become an endlessly flexible, improvised dance in which interviewers clumsily contribute with only a vague understanding of their role and the ideal outcome. The last time I was interviewing candidates, I felt exceptionally prepared when I spent thirty minutes reviewing a candidate's resumé and jotting down questions. It was better than nothing, right? Wrong. I hadn't discussed our hiring criteria with anyone else in detail, I didn't know what we had already asked other candidates, and my sense of the evaluation "framework" was a simple hire or no-hire decision.

I've talked to a few companies who have implemented scalable and robust interview processes. What do these companies do differently? They have one process that all teams use, for every interview. These hiring teams have set a certain number of interview rounds, and know exactly what needs to be evaluated during each round. Because the process is stable and consistent, they are able to train interviewers and people are able to join interview cycles seamlessly. In these systems, managers and hiring teams have some discretion to make small tweaks, but don't make significant changes without approval. To scale and maintain such a process, there is significant documentation to ensure all corners of the organization understand the process and rationale.

But less than a quarter of companies have even attempted implementing this type of system for hiring. This lack of process results in chaos, confusion, and inefficiency, but also leads to bias and bad hiring decisions. When there isn't a clear process or framework, employees fall back on their own instincts, which are rife with bias. Think of these biases as cognitive shortcuts that we rely on when there's nothing else to guide us. In the absence of a framework, this is natural, and we all do it. But in the hiring process, relying on instincts leads to you to apply these common biases that hurt your team's diversity:

- *Halo Effect*—when an impression created in one area (for example, an impression of someone's appearance) influences our opinion of that person in other areas. When interviewers judge candidates based on details like their handshake, clothing, or posture, they are falling prey to the Halo Effect, which tempts us to use irrelevant pieces of data to draw a broad conclusion about someone.
- *InGroup Favoritism*—when we favor members of our own group over others. This bias drives us to favor candidates from our hometown, alma mater, race, or other social group. This is an extremely common and powerful type of bias. According to an SHRM survey from 2015/2016, most employers get 80–90% of hires through referrals, which by design are recruits from our existing social groups.
- *Stereotyping*—when we apply a rigid and oversimplified, yet widely accepted, assumption about a group to an individual member of that group. We're stereotyping when we assume young people are more technically savvy, Asians are more analytical, or women are more kind.
- *Group-Think*—when we make a hiring decision as a team, but conform or agree with each other to avoid dissent and individual responsibility. When there's no framework for hiring decisions, members of the hiring team may fear speaking up and disagreeing with the group, which buries potential risks or advocacy for untraditional candidates.

These biases are so common and natural that it's not a question of whether they are present in *your* hiring process.

They most certainly are. Instead, the question is whether you have processes in place to help your team see, manage, and avoid using them to make hiring decisions. Without a framework and process to rely on, the hiring team will naturally fall back on these cognitive shortcuts, which will undermine your diversity goals. In January 2017, *Bloomberg* reported that Facebook was having difficulty hiring women and minorities, despite a well-funded and targeted recruiting strategy that included generous incentives for recruiters. The problem at Facebook was bias in the interview process: under-represented applicants were invited to interview but were not evaluated fairly. No amount of investment in recruitment of diverse candidates could overcome the bias those candidates faced in their interviews.

Beyond hurting team diversity, hiring based on these biases increases the risk of making bad hires generally. According to a 2017 CareerBuilder survey, 41% of companies said bad hires could each cost them $25,000, and another quarter of companies said the cost was over $50,000 per hire. The only way to avoid this impact on your business is to intentionally build systems and processes that create guardrails for your team in making smart, well-supported hiring decisions.

NO DATA: THAT WHICH IS NOT MEASURED DOES NOT IMPROVE

Nowadays, almost everything is measured and tracked: from customer service, to user acquisition costs, to inventory turnaround. It's hard to find a process or department that's not collecting data to improve and optimize output. The one place that consistently lacks data is the hiring and interview process, where only 18% of companies who responded to my 2016 online survey said they track hiring data to drive improvements. Companies may have data on employee satisfaction, employee performance, and retention, but they almost never know the interview practices that best predict job success for their company. They rarely know how to identify the best interviewers, or the most effective interview questions for specific roles.

Of course, it's difficult to capture useful data without process. The problems are linked. If your hiring team is asking each candidate completely different interview questions, how useful would that data be? It would be impossible to compare candidates based on their answers to questions if those questions vary. But without the data, your hiring is unlikely to improve.

NO TRAINING AND PREPARATION: HIGH-STAKES SINK OR SWIM

Hiring is a high stakes endeavor that we trust people to do with absolutely no formal training, and often with minimal instruction and guidance. We expect people at all levels of the organization to interview job candidates effectively and to know how to make hiring decisions. Is this a skill people are born with? Without training and education, people create their own methodology, riddled with bias and ego, and only loosely correlated to hiring success. This is what's going on when people start to rely on a "favorite interview question." It's foolish to think one question will fairly and effectively evaluate candidates, regardless of role, and unique company requirements. This lazy habit reflects more on the interviewer's personal preferences than on a job candidate's fit for the role in question.

Lack of training results in interviewers thinking of the process as an "art" based on their personal styles, when evidence shows that it's a science: there is a right and wrong way to interview job candidates. When your team members are armed with the science and tools to conduct interviews based on proven methods, they begin thinking more deeply about what success means in the role, and begin holding themselves and each other accountable for hiring success. But they need their organization's support to get there.

HOW DO WE FIX THE WAY WE HIRE?

Managers know hiring is their most important responsibility, but it always ends up last on their list of priorities, behind the "real work." Managers need a framework and methodology that does the heavy lifting, so they don't have to. This system should be stable enough to consistently safeguard hiring decisions and interactions against natural human bias, yet flexible enough to allow teams to customize the candidate evaluation based on their intimate knowledge of the roles they're hiring for.

In this book, we'll introduce a system comprised of three straightforward steps to get you and your team to hiring success. Step 1 will set the foundation, teaching you how to use "Star Mapping" to collaboratively articulate the hiring criteria for your next hire. Step 2 will introduce a better way to design interview questions. Finally, Step 3 will provide a powerful, yet lightweight, scoring system for evaluating and comparing job candidates.

YOUR THREE STEPS TO HIRING SUCCESS

STEP 1: PREPARE YOUR STAR MAP

Star Mapping is the foundation for this approach to hiring. The exercise leverages product development methodology used to map new features against a product's user journey. But instead of using it to prioritize new product features, you'll use the framework to prioritize hiring requirements for an open position on your team. The real power of this framework is collaboration. Star Mapping requires you to pull together a cross-functional team to collaboratively decide which candidate attributes, or Factors, are most important for evaluating job candidates. This collaboration reduces bias by creating accountability and intentionality, while also establishing shared understanding of the team's standard for a hiring decision.

STEP 2: DESIGN YOUR INTERVIEW

After your team clearly articulates what you're looking for in your new hire, it's time to write interview questions. But traditional interviews are dead. The way most of us conduct interviews today, defined by a loose and highly personalized conversation, must be replaced by a more strategic and structured method. In this section, you will learn how to build questions for a structured interview, a practice supported by decades of empirical data. In this step, you'll learn what structured interviews are, and how to harness their potential in a fast-paced team environment. As with Star Mapping, it's best to build structured interviews with your hiring team. You will learn a simple three-part framework for writing structured, reusable interview questions. Writing and using structured interview questions is a proven tactic for better predicting job success and significantly reducing bias in your hiring process.

STEP 3: EVALUATE YOUR CANDIDATES

What happens during the actual interviews? Although using structured questions has been shown to reduce bias, layering on a well-defined candidate scoring system brings rates of bias near zero. You'll learn a simple scoring system that you and your team can implement the next time you interview a candidate. It's easy to remember and won't require you to interrupt the flow of the conversation next time you're conducting an interview.

HOW TO USE THIS BOOK

The foundational principle across all three steps in this book is one I learned in my work as a product manager: cross-functional collaboration consistently yields superior results. After you are done reading this book yourself, share it with your colleagues, because these are not changes you can implement on your own. Your team needs to buy in for you to see the method's benefits.

Although I encourage you to test drive and use the tools and frameworks as soon as possible, read the book all the way through before you roll up your sleeves. It's important for you to understand how the pieces fit together, and how they build on one another.

After developing and refining this framework, I worked with hiring managers, Heads of People, and Chief Operating Officers who were interested in training their teams to improve hiring. Most lead fast-growth startups and teams that are either in the process of scaling or have just reached that point. Companies and teams at that point face a heightened risk because they have to hire so many people rapidly, usually with limited process and infrastructure. Those are primarily the people I had in mind when writing this book. But the methodology can be used by small teams making just one or two critical hires, as well as by large enterprises filling out departments. The tools are flexible to allow you and your teams to customize the approach as you see fit.

At each step, I'll use a simple example about hiring a Product Manager to illustrate the recommendations more clearly.

STEP 1: PREPARE YOUR STAR MAP

As soon as you get new headcount approved, it's tempting to quickly generate a job description and post it on job boards as soon as possible. Most managers do this on their own, or collaborate with HR. But it's a task that always feels like a nuisance—it's at the bottom of your to-do list and you rush through it only after the "real work" is done. Managers try to save time by copying and tweaking job descriptions from other companies, or by following HR's lead. If we really thought job descriptions were critical tools for hiring success, wouldn't we spend more time on them?

The reason managers don't give job descriptions much effort is because they usually create these documents before thinking through what they need from the new hire. Managers assume they'll be able to refine their hiring criteria during the interview process, as they learn what the market has to offer by meeting real job candidates. In other words, managers start the hiring process with the assumption that it's okay to waste the candidates' (as well as their own!) time. They believe they'll be able to course-correct their way to the right criteria for the job... eventually. In today's fast-paced marketplace, can you afford to meander towards your next hire? For managers hiring innovation teams, this is an especially costly approach because they face a much more competitive talent market and must make decisions quickly.

By evaluating and articulating hiring criteria upfront using the Star Mapping methodology, managers focus in on what they need early, reducing bias and increasing the likelihood of hiring success. If you don't feel you are prepared to define your hiring needs, then you are simply not ready to hire.

WHAT IS STAR MAPPING?

A Star Map is a flexible framework that guides your team in defining the specific attributes, or Factors, you will use to source candidates and make hiring decisions. It helps you map what you want in a star hire and serves as the foundation of the three-step approach for upgrading your interview process. The Star Map allows teams to define hard skills, but also challenges them to consider the soft skills and diverse perspectives that define a star employee who could fundamentally transform the team. As you can see in table below, using our example of the Product Manager, the Star Map captures the nine most important Factors your team needs in a new hire, evenly balanced across three pillars covering tools, agility, and dimensions.

Besides providing a structure to ensure balance across the three pillars, the Star Map is also a tool to facilitate collaboration and shared understanding. It helps teams establish clarity by articulating, *as a team*, exactly what they are seeking in a new hire. Teams generate hiring Factors together, then discuss and prioritize those Factors. In this way, the Star Map ensures relevant stakeholders have a voice in setting the hiring criteria for a new team member. It would be extremely difficult to try to collaborate on this level using a job description.

The Star Map is a traveling and living document, designed to be shared with your organization. Once you've completed a Star Map with your team, you should share it with leadership, recruiters, and HR teams, as well as with members of your extended team. The Star Map should live in a place that's accessible to the whole company. It should be updated once the role it describes evolves.

WHAT ARE THE COMPONENTS OF A STAR MAP?

Think about the best people you've worked with: the people who delivered extraordinary output while elevating their colleagues. Those people consistently possess the right tools to accomplish their tasks, navigate challenges with agility, and bring unique dimensions to the way they work.

The Star Map framework is designed to identify these well-balanced stars. It's comprised of two facets: three pillars (Tools, Agility, Dimensions), and three Star Factors under each pillar. Let's review what these are and how they work:

» *Tools*—these are the tools of the craft. They are role-specific, measurable, and tangible Factors necessary to complete day-to-day tasks. You can think of these as the "hard skills" a candidate needs to have on day one. These Factors cover WHAT the employee would do in the role. For example, a Star Map for a Product Manager might include these Factors under Tools: feature prioritization, able to build a product road map, and able to design effective customer research.

- *Agility*—these are the intangible Factors that allow employees to navigate the people, communication, and leadership dynamics of a role. You can think of these as the "soft skills" that capture HOW an employee will perform the daily tasks of their role. For example, a Star Map for a Product Manager might include these Factors under Agility: manages executive expectations, creative problem-solving, and understands business objectives.
- *Dimensions*—this pillar challenges teams to identify the perspectives that are currently needed and missing on the team. Think of these Factors as "Culture Adds" that expand a team's perspective and give them the winning edge against competitors. This pillar is powerful in that it has the potential to connect diversity objectives to team needs and business value. By now, most of us realize the concept of "culture fit" in the hiring process is problematic. The notion inadvertently encourages teams to reinforce a team's pre-existing culture and demographics. Dimensions are the antidote. For example, a Star Map for a Product Manager might include these Factors under Dimensions: fluent in Spanish, advocates for needs of customers with

disabilities, and interest in building products for emerging markets.

Now that you understand the three pillars, let's discuss the Factors. Under each of the pillars are three Factors, or individual hiring criteria that a team prioritizes together. Each Star Factor should set a high standard for the job candidates. These should not reflect the job's minimum requirements, but should instead be the qualities that define a star. Be careful not to make your Star Factors too specific. Being too specific will narrow your pool of qualified candidates. Stick to broad attributes, rather than specific skills. For example, rather than requiring that candidates be "Excel experts," which limits your candidate pool by software and assumes that there's only one way to conduct data analysis, define your Factor as "Efficiently conducts complex data analysis."

This shift will help the team focus on what really matters, rather than qualifying or disqualifying candidates based on irrelevant "proxy" Factors that serve as a hopeful representation, like software preference. Other commonly used proxy Factors include years of experience and degree requirements. Hiring teams use these as proxies hoping they represent something else, whether it's professionalism, maturity, or other things that actually matter to job performance. Why not skip the proxy and spell out the stuff that actually matters to the team's success?

The three pillars represent the critical areas you should always consider when defining hiring criteria. Considering all three equally ensures you search for and hire a well-balanced star. When hiring, most managers emphasize Tools. Some also consider Agility Factors, but only rare outliers hire for Dimension. Considering all three pillars will give your team an edge in the market. This is how you identify stars.

WHAT MAKES A GOOD STAR FACTOR?

- It is concise and clear. Keep it short and precise!
- It is focused on a single attribute (avoid "and" in the description).
- It's broad enough to allow for the unique and unexpected.
- It directly contributes to job performance.

STAR MAPPING WITH YOUR TEAM

You should use your Star Map whenever you are hiring. But you don't need to create a new Star Map if you already have one completed for a position and that position hasn't changed significantly. When you need to create a new Star Map, schedule an hour with a cross-functional team of people who will be interacting with the new hire. Once you get the hang of it, Star Mapping should only take your team about thirty minutes. I encourage you to keep the group to 3–6 people. As you might expect, the bigger the group, the longer the process.

First, as the hiring manager, you'll set context for the team by giving them a brief overview of the job's primary responsibilities, level, and place within the organization. I recommend visually communicating these and displaying them on a wall so the team can continuously refer to them throughout the process. Keep this high-level, but include an example of a significant project this role will be responsible for executing.

EXAMPLE: Role Overview for a Product Manager
(created by Chief Technology Officer)

Key Responsibilities

- Will build and manage changes to the product roadmap

- Will be responsible for leading sprint planning meetings, helping teams prioritize features
- Expected to develop the business model and forecast growth of product revenue
- Reports to the CTO
- Will directly manage 2 junior product managers, and 1 designer

Example Scenario/Project
This product manager will be responsible for leading the development of our native mobile applications, which should be launched in time for our conference this fall.

Next, the team will individually brainstorm the "Factors" they think are important across the three pillars. I recommend using sticky notes and markers to help people keep Factors concise, with one to a sticky note. Each member of the team should generate as many Factors as possible, and at least a few Factors for each pillar. Limit this brainstorming session to 15 or 20 minutes, then post everyone's Factors so the whole team can gather, read, and discuss them together. The goal of this discussion is to ensure the entire team has a shared understanding of each Factor, so people should feel free to ask one another to clarify the Factors they posted. This, though, is not the time to discuss the value or validity of each Factor. Instead, everyone should just seek to understand. During this time, the team can also group Factors that are repetitive and rewrite other Factors for clarity.

Finally, after ensuring everyone understands each Factor, each person will vote for the Factors they think are most important for job success in the role. Depending on the number of Factors and people, each person should get 2–3 votes under each pillar.

After everyone votes, the team needs to discuss and build consensus about the three most important Factors under each pillar, in no particular order. *It's this discussion that drives the most value in this process.* Remember these principles during these discussions:

> *Collaborate.* Star Mapping is only effective if it *adds* voices to the hiring process. As your team members present their Star Factors to the team, remember that each person needs to be heard and should be allowed the space to share and explain their perspective.
>
> *Diverge, then converge.* Star Mapping creates a more democratic process by allowing members of the hiring team to *diverge* by brainstorming freeform on their own. It is this process of divergence that will drive new ideas and insights and improve the hiring process by surfacing unexpected criteria. The team will eventually *converge* by prioritizing all the Star Factors together.

Star Mapping is the step that most surprises and excites managers. They are thrilled and shocked that their team has such insightful contributions for the hiring process. But managers have to guide this process carefully to arrive at these results. As the hiring manager, it is your job to ensure the people invited to the Star Mapping process bring diverse cross-functional perspectives and a deep understanding of the role you're filling. Star Mapping participants should also be people who will rely on the hire, and are therefore invested in the new hire's success.

STAR MAPPING FOR DIVERSITY

As I've mentioned a few times now, using a Star Map will ensure your team does not undermine your team's diversity goals. The process does this by helping you focus on WHAT Factors you need for success in the role, instead of WHO might be a good fit. This is important because we often try to hire people in the mold of others we've enjoyed working for in the past, a common hiring practice called "pattern-matching." The problem with pattern-matching is that we often fixate and match attributes that don't really matter for success, but exclude large groups of (often underrepresented) people. For example, venture capitalists in Silicon Valley are known to pattern-match for entrepreneurs who resemble Mark Zuckerberg: young white men who write code and dropped out of prestigious universities. Star Mapping pushes hiring teams to define broader, more relevant Factors that are more explicitly inclusive.

The reason why Factors on a Star Map are less biased is because the team discussions create transparency and accountability. In the Mark Zuckerberg example, if someone on the team had added "college drop-out" as a Star Factor, their teammates would likely challenge the importance of this factor: why is this critical to job performance? Could we imagine a college or high school graduate performing the job equally well? The person who wrote that Factor may clarify that they actually wanted to optimize for "entrepreneurial" or "risk-takers." These are Factors that are more inclusive, and depending on the role, more direct predictors of success.

In this way, diversity objectives are baked into every part of the Star Map: under every pillar and in each Factor. But teams that want to take their commitment to diversity a step further can do so by explicitly articulating diversity criteria under the Dimensions pillar.

GETTING THE MOST OUT OF YOUR STAR MAP

After you and your team complete a Star Map, be sure to capture the results as a living document. Don't let the Star Map die in the room you created it in.

Share the Star Map with all stakeholders, especially your leadership and recruiting teams. Executives should have a sense of the hiring criteria being used to fill key roles, and recruiters should use the Star Map to write a job description and refine candidate targeting. For example, if the Star Map calls for "entrepreneurial" candidates, the recruiter may decide to specifically target entrepreneurship Meetups or offer finders fees to bloggers who are influential on the topic. The extended team who will be working with this person should also be able to access your hiring criteria.

Another important reason to capture and record the work that comes out of Star Mapping is that you will probably hire for the same or a similar role again. At that point, you'll want to reuse your Star Map, if the role hasn't changed significantly, or refer to it to refocus the role or refine the recruiting process.

PRINCIPLES TO REMEMBER...

» Defining your hiring criteria should not be something you do alone. *Hiring is a team sport.* Even if you don't use Star Mapping, you can quickly transform and elevate your process by simply pulling a team together to help you jot down hiring criteria before you build the job description.

» It's important to build *shared understanding* with your hiring team before they conduct interviews. Everyone should agree and know what you're looking for and how you will each identify it.

» Bringing more voices into the hiring process tends to expose and eliminate potential bias. Team members hold each other accountable, ensuring hiring criteria is relevant and fair.

FAQ

What should our team do if we disagree on which pillar to put certain Star Factors?

» There is no right answer about which Pillar a Factor should be under. It depends on the company, the team, and the nature of the position. So if there's a disagreement, either take a vote or leave the Factor under both Pillars until you're done discussing all other Factors, then come back to them after gaining that perspective. But make a decision and move the Factor to one pillar before you begin prioritization.

Where do diversity Factors fall? Should we have them on our Star Map?

» Some teams choose to focus on diversity Factors in their recruiting efforts but leave them off the Star Map. That's okay, but I encourage teams that are extremely committed to increasing diversity to articulate that on their Star Maps, under Dimensions.

How can teams customize the Star Map for their needs?

» Some teams choose to extend the Star Map to four pillars, often making "diversity" a separate pillar of its own. This allows them to explicitly state aspects of demographic diversity they need on their team, while also articulating other types of perspective under "dimensions." That's okay, although I recommend adding one column at most to keep the number of hiring Factors focused and manageable. I've also seen teams customize a Star Map by relabeling the pillars using language that's more organic to their cultures, and I've seen teams use the Star Map for other types of decision-making, beyond hiring. All is okay!

STEP 2: DESIGN YOUR INTERVIEW

Traditional interviews are those unplanned, unfocused conversational interviews we've all participated in. They are usually guided by a few quick notes scrawled down by the interviewer a few minutes before they meet the job candidate. Because such minimal planning goes into these interviews, the interviewer often realizes after the interview that they didn't get all the information they needed to make their decision.

You know it's a traditional interview if it starts with "Walk me through your resumé" or "Tell me about yourself." In study after study, these types of interviews have proven ineffective in predicting job performance, and have been shown to be extremely biased. According to a study conducted by Michigan State University and published in the journal *Personnel Psychology*, traditional interviews can only predict job performance 14% of the time and, on average, women and minorities receive 20% lower scores from interviewers using this approach. With that kind of failure rate and bias, you're better off hiring people by choosing resumés at random.

GENERATING STRUCTURED INTERVIEW QUESTIONS

Instead of traditional interviews, you and your team should conduct structured interviews. A structured interview consists of pre-written interview questions, asked to all candidates in the same order. The goal of structured interviews is to create a consistent and level playing field across all candidates, allowing interview teams to easily assess and compare candidates fairly. Structured interviews have proven more effective than other interview methods in studies dating as far back as the 1940s. According to Michael A. Campion and David K. Palmer, researchers from Purdue University and University of Houston, respectively, "few conclusions have been more widely supported than the idea that structuring the interview enhances reliability and validity."

The structured interview method attempts to de-emphasize irrelevant factors such as a candidate's charisma, appearance, and personal chemistry, attributes which often unconsciously drive hiring decisions. If those traits are important to job performance there should be specific questions to assess them. The objective of the interview is to gather data towards an analytical decision.

We are most vulnerable to our biases when we turn analytical decisions into personal and emotional ones. Neither you nor I can help but be affected by a job candidate's fantastic sense of humor, polished appearance, or shared hobbies. Structured interviews help you remain laser-focused on the Factors relevant to job performance by preventing you from inserting those types of sentiments and bias into the hiring decision. According to studies published in the *Journal of Occupational Psychology* and in *Personnel Psychology*, not only are structured interviews twice as effective at predicting job performance, but they also reduce bias by half.

But managers and interviewers are understandably hesitant to try out structured interviews. They fear structured interviews are too time-consuming to create and don't allow as much control and improvisation in the interview. Above all, managers are afraid structured interviews will feel unnatural and strip away their own personal touch when speaking to job candidates. These concerns are valid.

Although they require an upfront investment in time, structured interviews have been shown to save teams at Google an average of 40 minutes per interview process. Interviewers won't need to spend time brainstorming questions individually and hiring decisions will be made more quickly and confidently.

Generating structured interview questions can be a challenge. To simplify it, I've deconstructed the process by identifying and isolating the three parts of a powerful interview question. Each question should have *Context, Question,* and *Follow-up*.

» *Context*—this is the "set up" for your question. This is an opportunity to anchor your question in scenarios that matter to you, your team, and your business.

It also provides the job candidate a peek into a real-life situation on your team. The situation you use for Context doesn't have to be real or current, but it should approximate a real or past challenge that your team encountered.

» *Question*—this is obviously the most critical of the three components. Each question should be tightly associated with a Star Factor from the Star Map you generated with your team. The question should focus on only one Factor. In interviews, we often make the mistake of trying to measure too much at once by asking multi-part questions. Instead, write a simple and focused, yet open-ended, question that will allow you to assess just one Star Factor thoroughly.
» *Follow-up*—these are always optional, and should only be asked when an interviewer does not feel they extracted sufficient information to assess the candidate's initial answer. You should only follow up in order to dig deeper or clarify the candidate's answer to the question. Strong follow-up questions come in four types: WHO (to dig into how the candidate worked with others), WHY (to explore the rationale and strategy behind their approach), WHAT (to focus on specific pieces of a plan or process), and HOW (to clarify the approach they used in a scenario).

Follow-ups allow room for the free-flowing conversation we all crave. But structured questions give all candidates the same opportunity and starting point for those conversations. Some candidates will provide rich answers, ask questions of the interviewer, and elevate the conversation, while others might give flat, superficial answers. The structured questions themselves don't prevent great conversation, they simply give every job candidate the same access to those conversations.

EXAMPLE: **INTERVIEW QUESTIONS FOR A PRODUCT MANAGER**

STAR FACTOR		
Able to design effective customer research	***Manages executive expectations***	***Advocates for the needs of customers with disabilities***
Context: We are considering giving users the ability to text our customer support team. *Question:* We are not sure if this is something customers would use or find valuable. How would you go about finding out? *Follow-ups:* **Who** would you target for this effort? **How** would you incorporate your learnings into the product?	*Context:* You realize that an important feature will not ship in time to hit a set of goals already communicated to the board. *Question:* How would you manage this with senior executives and the board? *Follow-ups:* **How** do you manage expectations for new products, when there are many risks and unknowns?	*Context:* We've discovered that a growing segment of our users has trouble seeing the details on their mobile devices. *Question:* How would you change the product based on this discovery? *Follow-ups:* **How** would you learn about the needs of this user segment? **Why** is this important or unimportant, relative to other product priorities?

You should only evaluate three Star Factors during each round of your interviews, for an ideal three interviews total for each candidate.

BENEFITING FROM COLLABORATION

You'll notice that the process for collaborating on questions is very similar to the one for Star Mapping. As with Star Mapping, bringing in more voices and perspectives will improve the quality of your output. Your hiring team will generate more creative and effective questions for the interview process if you do this exercise together. Collaboration is a powerful tool for all teams, but it is absolutely essential for teams who have the goal of producing innovative products and ideas. For these teams, collaboration must permeate all aspects of operations, not just product development. Of course, this also includes all steps of the interview process.

To start, as a team, choose three Factors that make sense to evaluate during a 1:1 interview, which can be a screener or other later-stage conversation.

Next, individually generate 1–3 questions for each of the three Star Factors you'll evaluate during this interview. It's important to time-box this exercise to about 15 to 20 minutes and remind participants that each "question" consists of three parts. So each person should generate 3–9 questions, each with three parts, depending on how much time you have.

Finally, post all the questions the team generated and place them so it's clear which question goes with which of the three Star Factors. Now, just like you did during Star Mapping, the team will review the questions together, then vote on the best one for each Star Factor. You may notice strong similarities in the questions the team generates. That naturally happens to teams once they've established strong shared understanding during Star Mapping.

Once you've finalized the questions for the interview, you should save and reuse them. Eventually, your organization should have a repository of interview questions that have been collaboratively generated and contain the three-part structure.

DESIGNING YOUR INTERVIEW PROCESS

After you've created the three questions for three factors, you're ready to conduct the first round of interviews. When accompanied by follow-ups, three substantive questions are enough for each round of interviews. If you have extra time, give that time to the candidate to ask their questions. Be sure to note the questions they ask in case you want to score the quality of that discussion in your evaluation of all candidates.

With nine Star Factors from your Star Map, you should plan to conduct three rounds of interviews, evaluating three related Factors during each interview. According to a study conducted by Google, you should need at most four rounds of interviews before making a hiring decision. If you're finding that your team requires additional rounds, it's likely that your hiring criteria are weak or unclear. In that case, you should revisit your Star Map to refine your process.

Assign one interviewer for each round of interviews. This is ideal, but if someone needs to sub in for some reason, the structured interview is designed to accommodate this since the questions are laid out to ensure all interviewers cover the same ground with each candidate. For each round of interviews, assign the interviewer who is most versed on the areas covered. For example, if you're interviewing software engineers, an experienced or senior engineer should cover the technical Tools discussion, while a project or product manager could evaluate Agility and a senior executive could assess Dimensions. It's up to each hiring team to identify the appropriate person to evaluate each set of Factors.

EXAMPLE: INTERVIEW PROCESS FOR A PRODUCT MANAGER

INTERVIEW ROUND	FACTORS ASSESSED	INTERVIEWER
Round 1 (Screener)	» Fluent in Spanish » Understanding business objectives » Interest in building products for emerging markets	Recruiter
Round 2	» Feature prioritization, » Building a product roadmap » Understanding business objectives	Product Manager
Round 3	» Able to design effective customer research » Advocates for needs of customers with disabilities » Fluent in Spanish	Senior Designer
Round 4	» Managing executive expectations » Creative problem solving » Interest in building products for emerging markets	Chief Technology Officer

As you can see in this example, the Factors for each interview are pulled directly from the Product Star Map. This team has opted for four interviews, with a screening interview conducted by a recruiter and confirming the candidate has a set of three essential skills that will also be assessed by the team during the subsequent three interviews. You may notice that each interview pulls Factors from more than one pillar. That's okay, as long as the team decides the three Factors are related and can be better assessed together.

OPTIMIZING YOUR HIRING EXPERIENCE

Once interviewers are assigned and scheduled, it's time to conduct interviews. When interviewing candidates, keep the following in mind.

- *Reframe the process.* A mistake I often see interviewers make is approaching job candidates as competition, as adversaries, or as imposters. There's no tool or framework that can change this mentality: this is often a result of a company's hiring culture, which is set by managers and leadership. To avoid or correct this culture, managers and executives need to lead by example by demonstrating an optimistic, supportive, and empathetic posture towards job candidates.
- *Communicate proactively.* Before and after each interview, your team should communicate proactively with job candidates. Let them know what to expect, what's next, and whether or not you have come to a decision. In my 2016 survey of job seekers, lack of communication was their top frustration with job interviews. I recommend assigning one person to manage the process of communicating with and updating all job candidates.
- *Avoid illegal topics.* It's extremely important that interviewers are well-versed on topics that are forbidden to discuss in job interviews. In the United States, these topics are governed by the Civil Rights

Act, Americans With Disabilities Act, and by state laws. State laws change often and the team needs to check state resources regularly to stay up to date. For example, in New York and California, employers can no longer ask job candidates about previous salaries. These types of laws are common in countries around the world, each with their own nuance and cultural emphasis. U.S. teams can review Federal Laws Prohibiting Job Discrimination Questions and Answers here: https://www.eeoc.gov/facts/qanda.html.

» *Compartmentalize chemistry.* As noted earlier, the key to fair interviews is consistency from candidate to candidate. But this is difficult because we're human and our feelings get involved: we click with some candidates or find others cold. As an interviewer, it's your responsibility to acknowledge this, its potential to impact the way you evaluate candidates, and interrogate its role in your hiring decision. When making a hiring decision, teams often bring up personal chemistry as a positive attribute for a candidate. Instead, teams should discuss this as a potential source of bias and ensure the hiring decision is not affected by irrelevant personal feelings.

» *Capture notes.* During each interview, interviewers should take meticulous notes. These notes should be used to provide support when making hiring decisions, but should also be saved by the hiring manager or HR in case any litigation risk arises. Putting thoughts and observations into writing helps interviewers become more self-aware, but also holds them accountable for their hiring decisions.

PRINCIPLES TO REMEMBER...

» Traditional interviews are useless. Studies have shown that on average, they predict job performance only 14% of the time.

» Structured questions provide a level playing field for candidates by creating consistency in interviews. Ask candidates the same questions, in the same order.

» Even if you don't implement structured questions, at minimum, make sure each question you ask is tightly tied to job performance. Especially when asking "culture" questions like "What do you do in your free time?" How well will their answer predict their success in the job? And might the question disqualify talented candidates?

FAQ

Can I bring a note-taker when I conduct a job interview?

» Yes! If you can coordinate with another member of your team, I highly recommend this tactic. One person can focus on asking the structured questions and follow-ups, while the other person simply takes notes and rates the candidate's answers as they are given. This is also an excellent way to create accountability and an opportunity for feedback in your interview process.

Won't job candidates be taken aback and uncomfortable with structured interviews?

» Job candidates are not startled when they are told ahead of time that they will be doing a structured interview, and when the team explains what a structured interview is and how it benefits job candidates. Studies have shown that job candidates tend to view structured interviews as more fair to them than traditional interviews. One study published in *The Journal of the Royal Society of Medicine* showed that 76% of job applicants perceived a structured interview process as more fair and 59% said the process enabled them to better demonstrate their strengths.

Do follow-ups need to be mapped out ahead of time?

» Although follow-ups don't necessarily need to be mapped out ahead of time, recording potential follow-ups for each question during interview design increases consistency and reliability of the process. Work with your team to define 2–4 follow-ups for each question using the WHY, HOW, WHAT, WHO framework to probe a candidate's answers only when their initial response doesn't provide enough information for you to confidently rate them. In your notes, jot down a reminder so you can share your follow-up with your team if it's necessary to explain your rationale for your scoring of the candidate.

STEP 3: EVALUATE YOUR CANDIDATES

Most managers make the mistake of running job interviews without a decision-making framework. They ask interviewers for unstructured feedback on job candidates. They rely on interviewers' memories and their ability to analyze a complex conversation, then reconcile that with vague hiring criteria.

This approach is deeply flawed. For starters, it's incredibly inconsistent. Each interviewer uses their own mental model to evaluate job candidates, and their standards fluctuate with each candidate depending on their personal tastes, moods, and biases. When interviewers finally huddle to give the hiring manager feedback on candidates, they spend much of the time trying to understand one another's mental models. This makes it impossible to compare candidates fairly. Observe the following example scenario, which most of us have experienced many times:

EXAMPLE: Hiring Team Feedback for a Product Manager
(a fictional scenario)

Amanda (Hiring Manager): Alright team, you've had a chance to meet Andy. What do you think of him? Is he a hire?

Micah: I'd hire him! He had a great attitude and he's seems really good at managing resources and timelines.

Marcus: Oh, I thought we didn't care about that stuff since Stephen has it covered under Project Management. I found him weak on professionalism and he seems to be most excited to work on data products, which isn't super relevant for our near-term.

Stephen: I agree with Marcus, he was unprofessional. But I'm impressed with his ability to run data analysis for marketing efforts.

Micah: But is *that* important? Doesn't Naomi already do pretty deep marketing analysis for the team?

Amanda (Manager): Hm. Well, looks like I'll have to make a call. Thanks for your input, everyone!

In the example, Amanda has to make a hiring decision. She's gathered feedback from the hiring team, who conducted interviews of the candidate. But their feedback wasn't very helpful because they weren't on the same page: each interviewer was using their own mental model for evaluating the applicant. Now Amanda must make a difficult decision with the somewhat scattered and inconsistent input from her team. No matter what decision she makes, someone on her team will feel their input was overlooked. The situation becomes even more fraught when a team is evaluating and comparing two or more job candidates.

As discussed earlier, groupthink adds another layer of bias to the hiring decision. Interviewers will tend to agree with the first person to state their opinion of a candidate, especially if the first person to speak up is the hiring manager or most senior person in the room. Without a framework, unique perspectives from the hiring team are muted or silenced. This defeats the purpose of having a diverse team weigh in and conduct interviews.

Finally, without a framework, when the hiring team discusses their thoughts on job candidates, nothing from those conversations is recorded and saved by the hiring manager or HR. Without this type of documentation, it's impossible to hold the team accountable for their hiring decisions. These teams cannot look back at previous hiring decisions to diagnose problems and make improvements.

USING ANCHORED SCALES TO MAKE HIRING DECISIONS

When there's no decision-making framework, bias fills the void. It's natural to fall back on cognitive shortcuts. To avoid this, your team should establish a framework and stop relying on unstructured hiring decisions.

What do we need in a framework to help us make effective hiring decisions? The framework should be consistent, simple, yet flexible. It needs to be consistent across the company so the resulting data can be aggregated and analyzed. The framework should also be simple enough to fit naturally into an interviewer-candidate conversation without demanding so much attention that it becomes disruptive. It should also have the flexibility to allow teams to customize their hiring standards.

Studies have shown that the most effective decision-making framework for evaluating job candidates is the anchored scale. Anchored scales offer the simplest and most scalable approach for scoring job candidates. Most people are familiar with the simple scale: often a 5-point scale used to rate almost anything, from food, to movies, to plumbers. The only difference between those and *anchored* scales is that anchored scales are labeled at each point of the scale—the "anchor" is the label. That reduces the subjectivity in the rating process and establishes shared understanding of expectations at each point of the scale: ideally, everyone knows and agrees what a 1 is, and how it's different from a 3 rating. When implemented effectively in the interview process, anchored scales have been shown to bring bias to almost zero, according to the aforementioned Michigan State University study about structured interviews. They are simple to use, and incredibly powerful.

THE 4-POINT HIRING SCALE

The 4-Point Hiring Scale is designed to simplify the interview process, while also reducing bias and driving efficiency in hiring.

The scale can be applied to each interview question or to an entire interview, and allows teams as much customization as they need.

BASIC 4-POINT HIRING SCALE

3 points	**Strong Hire**	Answers met and beat expectations
2 points	**Hire**	Answers met expectations
1 point	**No Hire**	Coachable, but did not meet expectations
0 points	**Strong No Hire**	Uncoachable and did not meet expectations

To evaluate Product Manager candidates on Star Factor "Able to design effective customer research"

CUSTOMIZED 4-POINT HIRING SCALE

3 points	**Strong Hire**	Expert knowledge of best practices, with ability to execute research plan end to end.
2 points	**Hire**	Expertly applies customer research best practices, can execute with light support.
1 point	**No Hire**	Knowledge of common research practices, needs significant support to execute or augment.
0 points	**Strong No Hire**	Little knowledge of customer research best practices.

As you can see, this scale has only 4 points by design: it forces interviewers to be decisive about whether or not to hire a candidate. There's no option to stay neutral.

There are two ways to use the 4-Point Hiring Scale, and each has a different level of efficacy. When the hiring team convenes to provide their feedback on a candidate, each interviewer provides their number rating (0 through 3) and explains their rationale, and everyone's assessment is recorded and scores are added together. This is the simplest implementation of the anchored scale, but it's also the least effective at reducing bias and improving hiring decisions because it continues to rely on interviewer recall and a single rating from each interviewer.

To get the full benefits of the 4-Point Hiring Scale, interviewers should score *each answer* the candidate provides, recording a score for each question asked. Then interviewers total the scores for all the questions to arrive at one score for each candidate. When the interview team convenes, then each interviewer has one score per candidate to submit and can articulate a rationale based on each of the candidate's answers to interview questions. This approach requires more effort, but is not necessarily less efficient if the team uses a simple scoring template during each interview. This is the approach that allows teams to drive bias near zero. That's because they are relying on real-time scores and notes instead of memory, which creates strong consistency and accountable. With this approach, it's important to warn job candidates that the hiring team will be taking diligent notes during the interview.

EXAMPLE: Hiring Team Feedback Using a 4-Point Hiring Scale

(a fictional scenario)

Amanda (Hiring Manager): Alright team, you've had a chance to meet Andy. What do you think of him? Is he a hire?

Micah: As you all know, I was evaluating Andy for Factors related to iteration and team management. He scored a 7 out of 9. He's the highest score we've seen in this area so far.

Marcus: Interesting. I conducted an interview with Andy focused on creative problem-solving. He scored a 3 out of 9. We haven't seen scores that low in this process.

Stephen: I assessed communication and client management. He also scored pretty low there—a total of 4 out of 9. Looking at my notes, he did well responding to client management scenarios, but I gave him a zero on communication because he kept saying transparency is overrated when sharing information with teams, an attitude that would be difficult to coach him out of.

Amanda (Manager): Okay, it doesn't sound like he'd be successful. Let's keep looking. Please send me your scores and evaluations of Andy so we can share them with HR.

In this example, the hiring team has learned their lesson and they're now employing a 4-Point Hiring Scale to help make and share their hiring recommendations. Notice the improved sense of clarity in their conversation: they have clear scores that can be used to draw comparisons, and they've taken notes to support their recommendations. Amanda, the hiring manager, can make her decision quickly and move the process along.

USING THE SCALE TO DECIDE

Although the scores gathered should be saved and used to make the hiring decision, they should be viewed by the team and hiring manager as a guide and not the final word. If a team or manager chooses to override or make a decision in opposition to candidate scores, then it's critical that they record the reasoning. In this way, the decision remains intentional, and captured for accountability. When HR or hiring managers review the strength of their hiring decisions, it'll be clear when teams chose to go outside the framework. Does this only happen for referrals, women, or other specific groups? Teams can use this documentation to evaluate and surface their own blind spots and biases.

USING THE SCALE TO ITERATE AND IMPROVE

As with every other operation, organization, or team committed to innovation, the hiring experience needs to be measured analytically, and improved continuously. The 4-Point Hiring Scale can reach further than applicant evaluation to attach actionable data to help improve every level of your hiring process:

» *Interviewer performance.* Over the long term, an interviewer's scores can be compared with a new employee's performance to identify the interviewers who most consistently predict applicant success. This method can also help to surface those interviewers who are less successful in order to provide them with additional coaching and support.

- *Interview questions and format.* Just as interviewer's scores can be compared to employee performance, the scores extracted from specific questions and interview formats can also be compared to employee value creation. Which questions, and which formats, correlate with employee success? The results of this analysis will help a team iterate to improve these evaluation tools.
- *Recruiting strategy.* If job candidates are consistently scoring low for specific Factors, then the problem may be that the recruiting resources need to be redirected to find more qualified candidates. The benefit of using Factors from your Star Map to refocus recruiting is that you can be specific about what attributes candidates need to have, and what they are currently missing.

PRINCIPLES TO REMEMBER...

- An anchored scale is simply a 4-Point Hiring Scale with labels at each point.
- Using anchored scales to score job candidates has been shown to drive bias to near zero. But to get these results, interviewers need to score candidates immediately after each question, rather than waiting until the end of the interview.

FAQ

How do we use and evaluate the scores?

» The team should total the scores for each candidate, then compare them. Some teams will set minimums and not hire anyone who doesn't score at least 7 points in each round or 20 points across three rounds of interviews.

How can we customize the 4-Point Hiring Scale for our needs?

» In the table above, you'll see that you can keep the default anchor labels, but you also have the option to define what the four points of the scale mean for your team. What you're doing by customizing the labels is that you're making the scoring more precise, explicit, and specific to your team and to the role you're hiring for.

CONCLUSION: BEYOND THE ONE-HOUR INTERVIEW

You are now equipped with the tools to design an effective interview process with your team. The three-step approach will help you elevate and standardize traditional interviews. But what about the other types of interviews, beyond situational and behavioral questions—the case studies, the portfolio walk-throughs, work samples, design studios, and many others?

After your team completes a Star Map, you're ready to consider the interview formats that best evaluate your Star Factors. First, group the Factors into three based on evaluation type—it'll be clear that some Factors go together, and should therefore be evaluated together. Now, consider the three types of interviews that will allow you to most effectively measure each group of Factors. The Factors should dictate the interview format, not the reverse. Do some Factors make sense for a screener phone call? Does one group of Factors require a case study? Does another group of Factors make sense for the final interview with the CEO? These are decisions you should make (preferably with your team), before you begin the interview process. When using methods such as portfolio walkthroughs, case studies, and the like, consider that not every personality type will respond well to performing on their feet. Unless that personality type is a Star Factor for you, be careful not to set applicants up to fail by surprising them during the interview.

Following these basic principles will help you improve the rigor and efficacy of any interview format:

» *Focus your evaluation.* In each interview, regardless of format, evaluate at most three Factors at a time, but choose an interview format that allows you to best assess the candidate for those Factors. Not every Factor requires that you ask the job candidate a question. You can evaluate some Factors simply by listening to a candidate work through a problem in a case study.

» *Keep it consistent.* No matter what types of interviews you conduct, it's important to keep them consistent from candidate to candidate. With each candidate, evaluate the same Factors so you can effectively and fairly compare each person. Set up the same scenarios, ask the same questions, and use the same scales for evaluation. Also, do your best to ensure the external conditions are uniform (phone versus in-person, location, interviewers, etc.).

» *Document and score.* Documentation is a practice your team should immediately implement, regardless of the approach you choose with everything else. Not only will it give you the data to improve your hiring process, but it will also provide support in a potential legal case. Scoring can also be used to improve hiring within any interview format—interviewers simply score candidates on a 4-Point Hiring Scale during every round of interviews. These are simple enhancements that could yield immediate gains in the form of improved decisions and process.

IMPROVING YOUR HIRING BRAND

> "I've learned that people will forget what you said, people will forget what you did, but people will never forget how you made them feel."
>
> —Maya Angelou

Using these tools and principles will help you improve the way you evaluate candidates. They should also improve your hiring brand. Most hiring managers and CEOs spend significant resources projecting a unique company culture when interacting with job candidates. They spend much less time thinking about their hiring brand, or what the interview and hiring experience is communicating to potential employees. The result is that companies may invest heavily in workplace amenities, but what stands out to candidates is that the hiring process seems repetitive, disorganized, or is marked by spotty communication that feels disrespectful. If you don't have a healthy hiring brand, other investments designed to impress candidates are made in vain.

The culture you're trying to sell to them isn't as powerful as the way you treat them during the process. Below are a few principles to consider as you think about the state of your hiring brand.

» *Communication.* Most job candidates are already familiar with the traditional approach to hiring. So if you're making improvements, be sure to give them a heads up ahead of time so they're not caught off-guard. It's important to communicate with your job candidates about how they will be interviewed, how they will be evaluated, and why this approach is important to you and your company. Even if the process is unfamiliar to them, this will reassure them the experience is intentional, thoughtful, and designed to set them up for success.

» *Transparency.* Your intent is to set job candidates up for success during the interview process, so share as much as you can without compromising the evaluation. Additionally, once you have documentation and scoring in place, you can consistently provide your job candidates with actionable feedback when asked.

» *Values.* How does your hiring process align with your company's values? This process is your first chance to show candidates how you and your team live your values. Remember this when designing your interview process. Choose interview formats that speak to your values and infuse those values into every candidate touch-point, including emails and other communications.

MAKING THIS A REALITY... START NOW

Where do you start? For a busy manager, already overwhelmed with the task of expanding your team, this might seem like a lot. But you don't need to make all improvements or do a full-scale, company-wide rollout at once. Start small.

If you only implement one tool, start with Star Mapping. The magic of Star Mapping is that it establishes the habit of collaboration, which is the most transformative element of this approach. Bringing more people into the process will make it more honest, more rigorous, and less biased. Star Mapping will also allow you to invite others in, which will create buy in for your hiring process, as well as for your hiring decision.

Share your wins and learnings. One of the benefits of this approach is that it's highly shareable: you can send a Star Map to your entire organization. The more you share, the more others in the organization will be interested and want to learn more about this new approach.

Finally, these three steps won't work exactly the same for every team and organization. It's up to you and your team to figure out what works for you, what doesn't, and what you may need to add, change, or remove. The steps are designed to be flexible, so make them work for you.

Now... get started!

READING LIST

This book either cites directly or draws upon the following sources.

Alonso, Pamela, and Silvia Moscoso. "Structured behavioral and conventional interviews: Differences and biases in interviewer ratings." *Science Direct* (2017) https://www.sciencedirect.com /science/article/pii/S1576596217300427?via%3Dihub

Bock, Laszlo. *Work Rules! Insights from Inside Google That Will Transform How You Live and Lead* (2015)

Campion, Michael A., and David K. Palmer. "A Review of Structure in the Selection Interview." *Personnel Psychology* (2006) http://citeseerx.ist.psu.edu/viewdoc/download ?doi=10.1.1.218.9107&rep=rep1&type=pdf

CareerBuilder. "Nearly Three in Four Employers Affected by a Bad Hire, According to Recent CareerBuilder Survey." (2017) http://press.careerbuilder.com/2017-12-07-Nearly-Three-in -Four-Employers-Affected-by-a-Bad-Hire-According-to-a-Recent -CareerBuilder-Survey

Google Internal Research. *Guide: Use structured interviewing.* https://rework.withgoogle.com/guides/hiring-use-structured -interviewing/steps/read-googles-internal-research/

Huet, Ellen. "Facebook's Hiring Process Hinders Its Effort to Create a Diverse Workforce." *Bloomberg* (2017) https://www.bloomberg.com/news/articles/2017-01-09/facebook -s-hiring-process-hinders-its-effort-to-create-a-diverse-workforce

Kell, Harrison J., et al. "Exploring Methods for Developing Behaviorally Anchored Rating Scales for Evaluating Structured Interview Performance." *ETS Research Report Series* (2017) https://onlinelibrary.wiley.com/doi/full/10.1002/ets2.12152

Levashina, Julia, et al. "The Structured Employment Interview: Narrative and Quantitative Review of the Research Literature." *Personnel Psychology* (2014) https://msu.edu/~morgeson/levashina_hartwell_morgeson_campion_2014.pdf

Segrest Purkiss, Sharon L., et al. "Implicit Sources of Bias in Employment Interview Judgements and Decisions." *Organizational Behavior and Human Decision Processes* (2006) https://www.sciencedirect.com/science/article/pii/S0749597806000690

Society for Human Resource Management (SHRM). *A Guide to Conducting Behavioral Interviews with Early Career Job Candidates* (2016) https://www.shrm.org/LearningAndCareer/learning/Documents/Behavioral%20Interviewing%20Guide%20for%20Early%20Career%20Candidates.pdf

Tversky, Amos, and Daniel Kahneman. "Judgement under Uncertainty: Heuristics and Biases." *Science* (1974) http://psiexp.ss.uci.edu/research/teaching/Tversky_Kahneman_1974.pdf

U.S. Equal Employment Opportunity Commission. "Federal Laws Prohibiting Job Discrimination Questions and Answers." (2009) https://www.eeoc.gov/facts/qanda.html

Westwood, Mark A., et al. "Applicants regard structured interviews as a fair method of selection: An audit of candidates." *Journal of the Royal Society of Medicine* (2008) https://www.ncbi.nlm.nih.gov/pmc/articles/PMC2376273/

Wiesner, Willi H., and Steven F. Cronshaw. "A Meta-analytic Investigation of the Impact of Interview Format and Degree of Structure on Validity of the Employment Interview." *Journal of Occupational Psychology* (1988) https://pdfs.semanticscholar.org/8aba/c481bc6b1d32d19676e36625b97383ba6416.pdf

ACKNOWLEDGMENTS

This book came together with the love and support of my whole family, but especially my husband Jeff and our daughter Fiona. I am thankful for the encouragement, patience, and sage advice from the team at Sense & Respond Press. Finally, thank you to Sarah Caliendo, for your contribution in helping shape the ideas in this book. This book would not exist without each one of you, and I am grateful.

Starting at Microsoft, **NICOLE RUFUKU** has spent her career in strategy and product, helping entrepreneurs and Fortune 500 companies build digital products. As a Principal at Neo Innovation (acquired by Pivotal Labs), she led engagements from ideation to scale. Nicole has built startup teams from the ground up, both as a founder and as a consultant. She developed an interest in hiring and diversity from her own experience hiring talent to power agile teams for rapid innovation. Nicole now applies her product expertise through her New York-based consultancy called Bonsai, where she helps growth-stage companies improve their hiring success.

www.bonsaihiring.com
@nicolerufuku

47313847R00040

Printed in Poland
by Amazon Fulfillment
Poland Sp. z o.o., Wrocław